JABARI's DREAMY STAR

His Journey into S.T.E.M.
Science, Technology, Engineering & Math

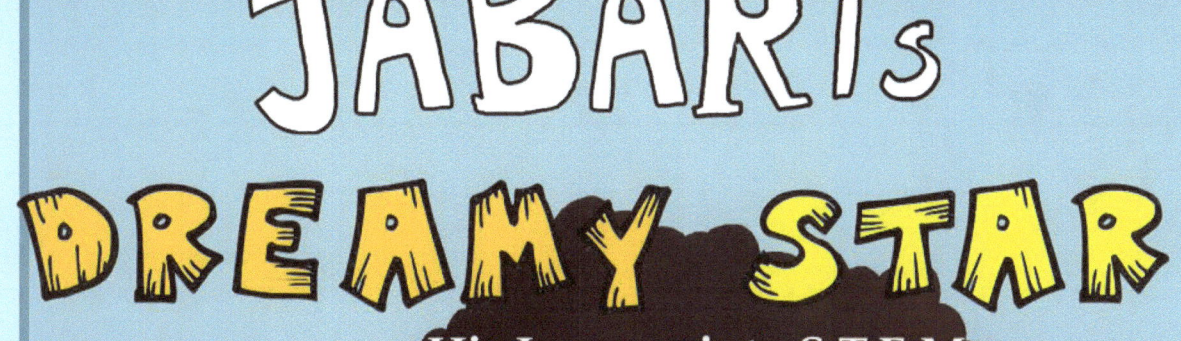

Written By
Erika Baylor & Jasmine Richardson

Illustrated By
Sanghamitra Dasgupta

Jabari's Dreamy Star by Erika Baylor and Jasmine Richardson

Copyright © 2023 Erika Baylor and Jasmine Richardson

Illustration Copyright © 2023 Sanghamitra Dasgupta

All rights reserved.

ISBN: 978-1-950861-72-9

Thank you for purchasing this book and complying with copyright laws by not reproducing, scanning, or distributing any part of it in any form without permission.

Published by His Glory Creations Publishing, LLC

Wendell, North Carolina
Printed in the United States

This book is dedicated to Stephanie Brown, mother of Erika and Jasmine, who always went out of her way to find activities for them to be exposed to within science, technology, engineering & math. She found a way to make summer fun and had hands-on experiences for them. She spent countless hours researching programs and driving them there.

Some secondary programs that stood out for Jasmine were a game design program at Drexel University one summer, and an engineering program at Villanova University the following summer. Erika thought that her most memorable program growing up was kayaking around the San Juan Islands off of the coast of Seattle, Washington studying micro ecology in middle school. Their mother found some amazing programs for them based on their personalities and interests.

Jabari is an African American boy who loves science! He knew this from the time he started school.

Jabari's preschool teacher, Mrs. Brown always told the class, you can be whatever you want to be.

One day during circle time every boy and girl stood up and told the class what he or she wanted to be.

Students said firefighter, police officer, doctor, clown, and then it was Jabari's turn. Mrs Brown said, "Jabari, what do you want to be?" Jabari stood up proud and said-- "I want to be a scientist!"

Mrs. Brown was proud of every boy and girl. Jabari was proud of himself! Over the years, Jabari worked hard in school, for he knew he needed good grades to be a scientist.

The next time a teacher asked students what they wanted to be, Jabari was in seventh grade. The teacher, Mrs. Johnson, asked who wanted to share. Jabari raised his hand proudly and said, "I'm going to be a scientist!"

Unlike preschool, the students said, "you can't be a scientist, you're African American!" The students laughed. Jabari sat down and looked at everyone. He had never felt this way.

Jabari went home and told his mom what happened at school. His mom gave him a hug, and told him he will be a scientist!

Over the next few years Jabari went to different science camps. He did robotics, dissected cow eyes, and was also introduced to an area engineering program, where he did hands-on engineering projects. With each program, Jabari knew his dream would one day come true.

At the end of ninth grade, Jabari's math and science teachers told him he could not register for the class that he needed. The teachers had another plan for the students that had brown skin like Jabari. Even when Jabari's family went to the school, the school would not allow Jabari to take the classes that he needed to take in high school for college.

Jabari's mom was smart. She told Jabari, "Do not worry, my prince. I have a plan." Jabari knew his mom had a plan, even though his mom did not share the plan with him. Jabari just went to school and never told any friends about his mother's plan.

Jabari went on and did his best in school. He continued to learn about all types of science, and attended Summer S.T.E.M. programs. He often won awards for his hard work. Jabari worked hard in high school while playing sports. Yet he still wanted to be a scientist of some sort.

Jabari applied for every opportunity that he could. One day when Jabari came in from playing, his Pop-Pop was waiting for him at the door. Jabari's Pop-Pop sat him down with proud tears in his eyes and told him about his day. He proudly said, "Jabari you had a phone call and they want to hire you as a Science Aide this summer." Jabari jumped up and down for what seemed like thirty minutes.

Jabari's mom reminded him, do not tell your school or friends. Everyone is not going to be excited about you being a scientist. This is all a part of our plan. That summer Jabari worked hard as a Science Aide, and learned all that he could.

Working as a Science Aide motivated Jabari to keep working hard in school, and to continue to be involved in his science programs outside of school.

Jabari worked as a Science Aide every summer until he graduated high school. At the same time his school continued to tell him that he would not be a scientist because he wasn't good enough in math or science, and he should find another major. Jabari went on to college and majored in science and math. It took hard work, motivation & dedication! After graduating from college, Jabari was hired as a scientist.

Jabari now encourages other boys and girls from around the world to go into science fields. He knows that many students are not encouraged to go into STEM, [Science, Technology, Engineering & Math] fields.

He wants to make the world a better place for all boys and girls! Jabari always knew that his family and pre-school teacher, Mrs. Brown, were right, you can be whatever you want to be! Dreams do come true!

Meet the Authors

Jasmine Richardson

Erika Baylor

Erika and Jasmine are sisters who grew up in Philadelphia, Pennsylvania. Both earned their Bachelor of Science degrees from the first Historical Black College & University, Cheyney University of Pennsylvania, one majoring in biology and the other chemistry.

Growing up these sisters were exposed and participated in many STEM activities that helped to shape them during their elementary and high school years. Some of their experiences included being active Girl Scout members, exploring the outdoors, kayaking, canoeing, dissecting, traveling adventurers to study science and high school level internships. These life experiences helped to guide them into their respective science fields.

Erika & Jasmine supported each other as they experienced some of the difficulties that women and black & brown people are subjected to within science. They wanted to use their experiences, positive and negative, to encourage other young boys and girls to believe in themselves. They hope that this book can be used as a motivational tool to inspire others who look like them to follow their dream.

Contact Information:
www.jabarisdreamystar.com

His Glory Creations Publishing, LLC is an International Christian Book Publishing Company, which helps launch the creative fiction and non-fiction works of new, aspiring and seasoned authors across the globe, through stories that are inspirational, empowering, life-changing or educational in nature, including poetry, journals, children's books, and recipe books.

DESIRE TO KNOW MORE?

Contact Information:
CEO/Founder: Felicia C. Lucas

www.hisglorycreationspublishing.com
Email: hgcpublishingllc@gmail.com
Phone: 919-679-1706
Facebook: His Glory Creations Publishing
Instagram: His Glory Creations Publishing
YouTube: His Glory Creations Publishing
TikTok: His Glory Creations Publishing

www.ingramcontent.com/pod-product-compliance
Lightning Source LLC
Chambersburg PA
CBHW050752110526
44592CB00002B/39